The Lotus

REALIZATION OF ONENESS

Vivian Amis

The Lotus

Copyright © 2015 by Vivian Amis

About the Author

Vivian Amis was born in 1961 in Germany and moved in 1994 to America. She is the author of *I AM - The Key to Manifesting*, *The Essentials of Life* and two children's books: *The Light within You* and *One Big Shine*. Vivian has written many articles and quotes on spirituality/self-help. Her articles have appeared in Spiritualnow, Wholistic Healing Research, Ezine Articles, New Times Naturally, Natural Awakening, Expressions of the Soul, Spiritual Living 360, and in Transformation. She lives with her husband, four children and two grandchildren in Tampa, Florida.

CONTENTS

"Apart from all beliefs, there is Truth."

—*Vivian Amis*

Introduction

In the eastern religions, the Lotus is associated with purity and beauty, which comes to the surface as a result of cleansing the mind and detaching one's true Self from the mind.

As a means of becoming the Lotus and the only way out of the murky water of suffering, we have created religions that may not be the shortest way to the desired destination. What is needed is an understanding that surpasses all scriptures.

What is needed are not more paths, but a way that is inclusive rather than exclusive, a path that is not a path toward our desired destination but a return to who we truly are before anything came into being. What is needed is a clear understanding of the principles that outline such a path so the seeker within all of us may return to its rightful place and the suffering in this world may come to an end. Then and only then will we know without a doubt that we are the sons and daughters of eternal life and the Lotus of purity and beauty.

Life

"If you don't know the question,
you are not ready for the answer."

Life, as most of us have come to know it, is a struggle between pleasure and pain. We have good days and we have bad days, which can be quite exhausting. We feel happy and we feel sad and then one day we awake to the question, Is this it? Is this all life has to offer us? When this question arises, the Guru shows up. The Guru may show up in the form of a person, a book or an experience through which we gain a greater awareness and we are invited to step out of the life as we know it and into the realm of spirit.

The realm of spirit is within you and it is present wherever you are.

Yet we are so busy with everyday life and events and trying to change others and our world that we don't see the beam in front of our own eyes. We try to change the world, yet our own house is in turbulence and divided. I don't mean just the physical house we live in, but our own temple or better said our own mind.

We recognize that we are suffering, but blame the world for our suffering. It is either the fault of our government, our parents, our neighbors or co-workers that we think we are unhappy and we may even come to the conclusion that life without all these people would surely be a happy one. If everyone would just leave us alone, accept us as we are, no longer have expectations and demands on us, then surely we would finally find peace within us and we would be happy.

But others are never the cause for our own inner turbulence. No one has the power to do anything to us unless we open the door through which it is possible and give them permission to enter.

It takes a conscious choice to be at peace or to be loving or to be happy in spite of things happening around us.

As much as others are not to blame for our experiences, they are also not the source of our peace, our happiness or our love. This is a realization that must first take place if we want to experience change, and this realization is the first step in going within to the true source of our suffering.

As we take the time and a closer look within ourselves, we start questioning everything. We start questioning our beliefs; what others have taught us and what we think we have learned from our experiences. We start asking questions that pertain to life, such as who am I and why am I here. We start questioning what we perceive and eventually realize that everything points back to the mind.

If we encounter a problem in our life, we worry, can't sleep and toss and turn all night until we finally at one point give up, and that is when the magic happens. The problem somehow disappears, dissolves on its own or we find a new way of accepting what is and make the best out of it. Aren't humans great? Somehow we always rise above.

Yet even further into our journey of life, we come to the awareness that in the absence of thought, we are actually at peace. This might not be a conscious realization, but those that are fed up with being out of control of their life look to see if there is something that could help us gain some control. We seek something that is constant, so life no longer feels like a yo-yo bouncing up and down. Somewhere down the road of life we develop hope and eventually are convinced that there is a way out.

Somehow we bought into the possibility of everlasting happiness apart from the world of things. This books aids in that realization, which must be realized by each one of us individually for a real change in our life and a permanent lasting effect to take place.

From the murky waters, let us therefore lift the "I" within each and every one of us to the full blossom of the Lotus.

The
Cause of Suffering

"All suffering is in and of the mind."

The cause of all suffering and only obstacle to realizing Oneness is the belief in a separation from God. God in this sense is our true essence and nature. God is not a person or image of our imagination, but the source within all of us that is alive and is life itself.

In order to be free of suffering, the true Self (which is God) must be detached from the mind and realize its true nature as being One with the absolute and as the absolute.

Within the mind we experience desire, attachment and fear. We have created a world of images that we have not only attached ourselves to, but have given a meaning to other than what they in reality truly are. The mind does not see things the way they are, but relates to them and gives them meaning. This is how we created a world of our own making and apart from what truly is in reality.

In this world "outside of God," there is the appearance and experience of separation. In this world outside of God, there is pleasure and pain.

It is the world of duality, believing in a separation from God and therefore creating an illusion of what we think this world is, who others are and who we ourselves are in relationships to all. In the world of duality there is you, me and God. We appear to be separate. In the world of duality, Oneness is broken down into parts.

In Oneness there is only One and all life is a part of that One. It is the totality rather than the individual manifestation.

God in this sense is the totality – the absolute and One, yet manifests in the physical realm threefold: The Father, the

Son and the Holy Spirit, also known as the Mind, the Heart and the Soul.

In Oneness:

1. The Mind is silent – this is the Father – Peace - The Creator
2. The Heart belongs - this is the Son – Love - The Demonstrator
3. The Soul knows its Self – this is the Holy Spirit – Joy - The Experience

In Separation:

1. The Mind seeks to know – We seek and form beliefs and concepts
2. The Heart wants to belong – We attach our heart to things, people and memories
3. The Soul wants to be – We claim to be this or that

In separation, we experience suffering.

Suffering through desire:

The belief in duality causes one to feel a hunger deep within us. This hunger is a feeling of lack, a hole that needs to be filled. Born into this physical world, seemingly separated from that which truly fills us and feeds us, we come to believe that physical things could fill the void we feel inside. This temptation is manifested within us as desire and which we substitute for the "real thing." The mind is sent out to seek and find and tries to understand that which is beyond the mind. This "seeking without finding" causes great frustration and anger within us. We are mad at ourselves, but since the mind is not turned inward and tuned in to the small inner voice, but rather out "there," we blame others or circumstances and situations for our misery.

Desire keeps us seeking because without that which we are truly seeking and the only thing that could really fill us, we are unhappy. We seek a relationship, a child, a house, a new car, an education, a great paying job, a title and so on until we one day realize that nothing in this world can truly fulfill us but keep us "hungry" for more. Things of this world can only make us temporarily happy.

Suffering through attachment:

Once we find something that makes us feel good and safe, our heart attaches itself to it. The heart that wants to belong attaches itself to things, people and memories of the past. The problem with this attachment is that since it is only temporary, you are in danger of losing it.

Everything in this world has a beginning and an end. Everything of this world is temporal. Let's say you desire a new car and finally get your dream car. You are happy, but that happiness lasts only a short time, for the minute that car disappears you are unhappy and suffering sets in.

Suffering through fear:

The belief in a separation from God causes fear. It is the belief in a life outside of God. A life that needs to be controlled, guarded, protected and managed. It is the fear of losing one's own life. This is what some refer to as the ego. The ego wants to live, and if we give up the control over our life, it will be out of control. If we don't guard our life and protect it, we will lose it. Who will do all these things if we don't? If we don't hang onto life, we will lose it.

The Seeker

"You seek Love,

Peace and Joy in this world...

But Love, Peace and Joy are

divine aspects of YOU."

Even though what everyone is seeking (consciously or not) is to realize their true Self, not everyone is ready to actually find their true Self. For in order to find your true Self, you have to give up the "fake" self, which kind of feels like dying. It is not a physical death, but a separation from the physical. This "fake self" appears and is often referred to as our ego.

Many on a spiritual path try to rid or kill the ego, but you cannot kill the ego nor ignore it. Since ego is the belief in separation, the ego drops away and disappears as a result of realizing Oneness.

The one who gives up their life (metaphorically) and goes beyond mind finds a peace not of this world, a love that is not conditioned and a joy unspeakable. Instead of dying, you awaken to Life.

Filled with a love so deep, so sweet that it hurts, this love is not attached to anything, has no demands or expectations but flows freely to all.

It is everything you ever hoped for and your search is over, for you have found. It is not difficult; rather, it is so simple that the mind can't grasp it, which makes it not only difficult but impossible to understand through the means of mind.

When the real Self is found or realized, the search is over. You may not have at this point all the answers, but you simply no longer have questions.

As mentioned before, some may not be ready to find the Truth and still want to experience the physical realm, and that is o.k. For unless you are ready to give up EVERYTHING, you are not ready for the Truth.

For unless you want the Truth more than the need to be right, more than any of your possessions, more than any of your memories, more than any beliefs you hold, more than life itself.... you are not ready for the Truth.

This is what Jesus meant when he said in Matt. 10:37, "He that loveth father or mother more than me is not worthy of me: and he that loveth son or daughter more than me is not worthy of me."

Unless you desire nothing more than to know the Truth, you are not ready for the Truth.

Yet to the true seeker that has an earnest desire to know the Truth, no path is needed, for the Truth will find YOU.

You are made in God's likeness and image: PERFECT, but you don't believe you are. You think you need to do something in order to be, but you are already. No one cannot "be." Everyone, consciously or not, is being someone. So the seeker meditates, does yoga, memorizes the scripture and goes to church, but none of these actions

actually bring you closer to God, for you are already One
with God. All these things only demonstrate the belief that
you are not already One. In other words, if you still think
you need to do something in order to be One, you are not.
Alone the thought that you are not, and already your Self
causes you to experience a less than perfect one.

You are already your Self. There is nothing you need to do
other than to realize this truth. You were your Self before
you were born into this so called life, but unless you are
consciously aware that you are already that which you seek,
it will not be your experience.

The separation never happened. The belief in a separation
creates the illusion and this belief is the only sin that exists.
It is the original and first lie and the cause of all other lies
and beliefs.

What is needed in order to realize you are what you are
seeking is a removal, an undoing, a radical surrendering, a
giving up and letting go.

Jesus realized his true Self by surrendering his mind, his
heart and his soul. From Buddha we know once a prince he
cut off his hair, left home, left his family and became a

monk. He meditated for six years, practiced self-mortification and extreme fasting, but did not achieve enlightenment.

Then finally, with a firm determination and belief without doubt, he sat down under a Bodhi Tree and was not going to move until he had reached his goal.

In Buddha's example we can see that no action on his behalf caused him to realize his true Self: not meditating, not fasting and not leaving home and his family.

Meditation can help quiet the mind, which brings about great peace, but in order to realize one's true Self, one has to move beyond mind.

Stop doing what you are doing. Stop seeking and realize that the only thing keeping you from experiencing Oneness is thought: The idea and belief in separation.

Thought is the only thing that separates you from Self, from God and from being One with all, and if you observe a thought, you are not that thought, but the witness to it. In separating your Self from the mind, you are at peace and your mind becomes silent. The awareness also arises that you are that silence.

Another apprehend hindrance from realizing Oneness, is the contradiction that only he who seeks will find, yet seeking you will not find. The seeker that seeks and finds is the one who has an earnest desire, determination and will not stop until he finds what he is looking for. He is ready to let go the minute the "aha" moment arrives and Truth shines through. On the other hand, the seeker that is seeking still in the world, yet not seeking for the sake of finding the true Self, but rather for the benefits that come with realizing one's Self, will never find. The very action of seeking is the demonstration of the belief that you have not found. For either you are seeking or you have found. You cannot have found if you are seeking. The validation of realizing Oneness is that the seeker is no longer seeking, for the search is over. What else is there? What else could be added to wholeness and completeness? What else could be added to the absolute? If it is the absolute, there is nothing that could be added or it were not the absolute.

The Seeker that seeks enlightenment for the sake of benefits that come with enlightenment is still seeking pleasure and fears pain, whereas the true seeker is ready to give up pleasure and is ready to do so, no matter the price.

Enlightenment to the true seeker is not a price or reward; it is a matter of life and death.

The Path

"There is only one path...

and everyone is on it."

It is said that there are many paths and it does seem that way. One person says do this and another person says do that, but no matter what happens, life itself is the way and shows us the way. We are pushed and pulled into so many directions and end up clueless to what we should do or what path we should take.

Please know that this too is a part of the plan, as everything is, for in a bigger picture your very life is your path no matter what path you seem to be taking. With other words you can't do anything wrong. You cannot ever be off the path no matter how hard you try. You could sit in your room and watch TV all day, and this would be part of your path. You could not believe in a God and be an atheist and you would still be on your path, because your life IS your path.

If you think, however, you have to walk on a path toward realizing your true Self, your path will become your hindrance. The sooner you get off your "path," the better and the closer you will be to your goal. What is needed is a step. Just one step, that's all. And the only reason why you need to take this step is because of where you are right now. If you want change to occur, you have to do something different. This "doing," however, is not what you think it is. It is an undoing, a return to, a stop doing. What you are doing is attaching the Self to things and people. What you are doing is buying into beliefs, concepts and ideas that are of this world and not based on the Truth of being. What you are doing is separating yourself from LIFE by believing you are your mind and body.

The only step you need to take is to surrender and let go and the rest will be taken care of. If you cannot surrender to God, surrender to a Guru. For God and Guru are the same and One.

The Guru

"Only a sincere devotee has
the ability of being lifted to
the status of the devoted."

What you are seeking in this world is to realize your true Self. Realization cannot be taught, nor can anyone do it for you, since it is You who realizes You.

Teachers, also known as Gurus, can point to your real Self and teach you where to find your real Self, but you are the one that has to take the steps of actually seeking and finding your true Self. No one can realize the Self for you nor can anyone give you this realization.

A Guru or teacher does not need to be a living person. It could be a master that already passed or a book you read on enlightenment. Nevertheless, the true Guru is within you, appearing outside of you as long as you believe in duality and seek outside of you.

There are pros and cons to seeking a physical Guru outside of you. The danger of seeking a Guru outside of you is that you could create a co-dependency and become dependent on a Guru. Some Gurus are still ego driven and seek power and may take advantage of their followers. On the other hand, it is easier to follow someone that has already walked before you and is there where you want to be. It could also mean a shorter time, and less obstacles to overcome before the Self is realized.

The sole purpose of a Guru is to point a student back to themselves. The Guru is a constant reminder to us that we are on a mission and not to cease from the mission until the goal is achieved.

In our everyday life it is easy to give up or become distracted from our goals. Our mind is all over the place and without a Guru we really are on our own to not just keep ourselves focused and motivated, but we have no one to bounce ideas off or ask questions that will arise during our journey.

A Guru has the ability to show shortcuts and knows the keen mind of a student and the traps the mind can play on us.

Even with our earnest attempts to conquer the ego, we may get off course or go astray, get lost and give up. Yet the Guru knows of these things and can avoid it from happening or guide us back onto the path so we may come to the finish line of our journey.

Gurus take on many different faces and appearances. Some may appear rich, others may appear poor. Some are male, others are female, some may be of radiant health and some extremely ill. Some may appear loving and some truly rude. Don't let the appearance fool you and don't judge the book by its cover. To get the full effect out of the disciple-Guru relationship, the student must learn to trust the Guru and follow the Guru.

In order to find the right Guru for you, look within you and look for signs, such as how you feel around them. Do you feel uplifted in their presence? Does their message make sense? Do they emanate peace/love/joy?

The key here is to surrender completely to the Teacher. If we cannot surrender ourselves we must surrender our life to the teacher and become disciples, for within the state of deep devotion the disciple is lifted beyond his own small self and into the realm where the teacher dwells.

The ideal student is the one that completely gives his life to the teacher and trusts only in him. He keeps a keen eye on his mind, so as not to let doubt separate him from the teacher, or the spell will be broken and there is nothing the Guru can do to mend it. Once the bond is broken, not only is the magic gone, but also the possibility of being lifted up and out of the illusion.

Knowing vs. Knowledge

"You cannot know your
real Self in terms of knowledge;
you can only know your
real Self by being 'it.'"

All knowledge is of this world and subject to change. Knowledge is information. This information is gathered from the outside, the world of form, and transmitted through your senses to the mind. All the knowledge in this world will not bring you closer to realizing your true self and serves only the purpose of learning belief systems that exist only within the physical realm of things.

As scientists are finding out more and more about the physical realm and how matter is more thought than truly physical, we come to the point where matter meets beliefs.

If Albert Einstein, who said that energy is matter, was right, then mankind must ask the question what is energy? Some think God is energy, since it cannot be created nor destroyed, but for me the question arises if God is energy then what is life? Life is not matter, as we know there is a difference between a body that is dead and a body that is alive. If there were no difference, I would agree with the possibility that God is energy. The body is energy and energy can still be measured after life has left the body, so my conclusion is that energy is the body, which is coherent with Albert Einstein's theory that energy is matter.

So where does energy come from, you may ask. My theory is that energy is the belief that there is a separation from God. It is the power of the ego creating a world of illusions. Without mind, there is no world. Without mind, there is only existence, life or what you may also refer to as pure awareness. For even when the body is sleeping and no thought occurs, we still exist. Even in deep meditation when the mind is silent and the world disappears, we do not cease to exist. There is something else governing our life.

With all the technology we have in our world today, one thing we cannot create is life. Life can only come from Life. You cannot create life from matter. So, who creates life or who created Life? This is where the concept of God comes from, and rightfully so, but it is not the God of religions but the God of Life, who is Life itself.

Some say God is consciousness, but consciousness is always about something. So what is Consciousness? Consciousness is the ability to perceive, which includes things we are aware of and things we are unaware of. In other words, it includes things we are conscious about and things we are unconscious about. Yet without mind we would not have that ability. So my conclusion is that consciousness is mind, and a divided mind equals the belief in duality.

When the mind is silent, as in deep sleep or meditation, there is no consciousness, yet we are alive and do not cease to exist. The Self ceases to exist and so does the world. The one who has separated his true Self from Mind is no longer aware of the world or a Self, but is fully aware, or as some may refer to it, "awakened." This is referred to as the state of enlightenment or Oneness.

Consciousness is a byproduct of awareness. Awareness is pure being-ness without being aware of being anything and not aware of anything. Awareness is life and existence, yet a silent existence void of objects. It is a knowing rather than knowledge of objects and forever within itself as the silent witness. Awareness is prior to consciousness. Awareness can exist without consciousness but not the other way around.

Life is pure awareness, from life the mind appears and from the mind the world appears and all objects in it. Awareness is always silent and in a no knowledge/no thought state. It is the Light of the body shining within itself when no objects are present within mind. This state of being is knowing without knowledge, for even though there are no objects, and because there are no objects, all light is retained within itself. It is being itself and therefore known as presence. It cannot be known in terms of knowledge, as all knowledge is about something. Pure awareness surpasses all descriptions, as it is beyond mind or better said before mind.

This is the pure mind, the innocence of a child we all were before anything came into being and still are behind the veil of unknowing.

Just like the rays of the sun illuminate objects that depend on the sun, consciousness depends on awareness for its existence. Consciousness is a byproduct of awareness or what some refer to as the Absolut, God or Self, but it is not the absolute. You are beyond.

Meditation

"Only in the silence of our mind are we One."

Meditation is a means of dispelling the illusion created by the mind. It is a tool one may use but without a true understanding of what meditation is, it's purpose and how to apply it the fruits cannot be gathered. You may find yourself meditating for many years without ever acquiring the desired results.

When Buddha became a monk, he meditated for six years, and even though he felt he got closer to his goal of realizing his true Self to bring forth the desired result, something was missing.

Buddha had the determination and true earnest desire needed to dispel the illusion, but what was missing was the final step: the surrendering.

Buddha, determined to reach enlightenment, sat down under the Bodhi tree and vowed not to move from the spot until he reached his goal.

Here we should note that Buddha was alone, not engaged with anything or anyone other than his own thoughts.

When we compare Buddha to Jesus, we see that Jesus was also alone while walking 40 days through the wilderness and tempted only by his own thoughts.

Meditation has been around for thousands of years. The reason why so many engage in this activity is because of the desired result this action brings about. The cause of suffering no matter if it is fear, worry, anger, jealousy, insecurity, stress, loneliness and desire, is associated with the mind. And to be exact, it is the associating WITH the mind that brings about these emotions.

Which brings us to the question: What is an emotion? An emotion is different than a feeling. An emotion is a reaction to a thought. Feelings are divine and completely independent of any "outside source." There are only three divine feelings and they are peace, love and joy. A spiritual master experiences these three feelings all at the same time, which is Bliss.

But back to meditation: Meditation is a tool to help one gain 1) control over the mind and 2) separate oneself from the mind and simply become a witness to the mind.

The mind is like a child who constantly wants something. It is screaming, "look at me" and wanting constant attention. It is screaming, "I want this" and "I want that." It is screaming so loud that we can't hear the small voice inside of us and it is screaming so loud that we can't hear, see, or observe anything that is truly going on around us. All of our attention is on this "child."

In order to truly change our life, be at peace and see the beauty all around us and hear that small inner voice that connects us with our true source, we need to first train the mind.

This is where meditation comes in and is a very helpful tool. Meditation is a practice of training the mind.

In order to train the mind, you may choose to set 15 minutes aside every day at the same time. This way you start training your mind and form a positive habit. Make sure you will not be disturbed by a phone going off. You may choose to lie down or sit, but if you get too comfortable you will fall asleep and miss all the action. If you set your meditation time of day to the evening, you are also more likely to fall asleep. So just try it and adjust to whatever and whenever works for you.

There are many ways to meditate, but what all of them have in common is the focus of mind on one thing. This "one thing" can be anything. Focusing on breathing is the easiest, least expensive and you have it wherever you go. Close your eyes and put your attention on breathing.

When a thought catches your attention, recognize it and bring your attention gently back to breathing. Keep doing this. This is training the mind to stay where you want it to be. With time it will get easier and fewer thoughts will have the power to pull your attention away from breathing.

When this goal is achieved, it is time to become aware of thought. This is a step that most people seem to miss and so stay with the practice of meditation for many years, never moving to the next step and never moving from that state of being to a higher state of awareness.

Meditating on one thing brings about great peace, for a mind that is cluttered with many thoughts about many things is exhausting. Our attention is pulled to every thought in all different directions, which causes anxiety. When the mind becomes one-pointed, things start to flow with ease and the light within us starts shining through. However, this state of being is not permanent and requires the constant practice of meditation.

The only true, lasting result happens after the second step in meditation takes place: the separation from mind.

It is easier to let go of the mind or, better said, separate from the mind when we are only dealing with one thought rather than a lot of thoughts.

One more thing should be addressed at this time. You may have heard of guided meditations, which engage with the hearing senses, meditating using your senses such as staring at mandalas, which engages the seeing senses, burning incense, which engages the smelling senses, or lying on a bed of needles, which engages the touch senses. The problem with using your senses to dismiss the illusion is that the senses are vehicles that bring information to the mind. No enlightenment can be achieved by using an outside source. It may bring about some peace and relaxation and aid to training the mind, but the effect is temporary. The illusion can only be dispelled when we go within and beyond the mind.

See the thought, try to grasp it with your attention and recognize it as a thought. Do not judge the thought as good or bad; it is just a thought. You are observing a thought and are no longer one with thought, but a witness to thought. Ask yourself: Who is witnessing this thought? Once you become aware of the witness, you are free to be and observe the perfection beyond thought.

Another way of meditating is through inquiry, either Self inquiry or Truth inquiry. Again the mind is focused on one thing but rather than on breathing or focusing on an object the focus is directed toward the mind. Self-inquiry is to ask the mind: Who am I? The mind will answer the question. The thought appears saying I am so and so and maybe it will be your name. Then you ask again who am I and the mind may say your age, your weight, your title, your job, your family status and so on. As the focus of attention remains on the question, the mind sooner or later has unraveled all the information it has acquired over time and it comes to the end of knowledge about who we think we are and becomes silent.

This silence is the result of the mind being empty of answers. It has given all the answers it could and knew of and surrenders because it does not know anything more. At this point the mind "gives up" and the real Self is revealed.

The same goes with Truth inquiry. Those coming from a Christian/Catholic background and taught by Jesus to know the Truth, which will set us free, may feel more inclined to seek this form of meditation. Even though Jesus said these words thousands of years ago, only very few have ever really asked the question what is the Truth? The inquiry for Truth will reveal the Truth beyond the illusion on duality.

The Self

⌒⌒∞⌒⌒

*"You are not who you think you are nor
anything your mind can come up with."*

The real Self is beyond mind. It is not a state of being, as all states of being are within the mind.

The thoughts of "I am this" or "I am that" appear within consciousness and even though you are conscious, your real Self is beyond consciousness. We use words to communicate, but words cannot describe that which is beyond consciousness. We have given words meaning and even though they serve a purpose here in this world, they are limited to our understanding.

The Self that you are seeking is not the one you portray to the world or go by in this world. If I asked you who are you, you would probably answer I am so and so and give me your name. That is usually the first way of identifying ourselves and what identifies us to be the person we are. If that identification is not enough and depending on the circumstances, you would maybe add your age, your title, your family status and so on. But all these things make up a person and even though you are that person, that person is subject to change. The Self you are seeking to remember/connect to or realize is that which is constant and unchanging. If you knew yourself to be your name, would you cease to exist if you changed your name? If you knew yourself to be a mother, did you not exist before you had children?

The real Self is ever there but lets ego run with the belief in being this or that until it no longer serves you and you go within to find out who you truly are.

When all titles of Self are dismissed, one realizes that I am not this or that and the "I am" stands alone. You may not know who you are in terms of knowledge, but you know you exist. The real Self is pure being-ness without being anything in particular.

This is the true Self, yet still appearing within Consciousness. Beyond consciousness is nothing, yet it is everything.

Another beautiful contradiction. How can I be nothing and everything at the same time, you may ask. Well, nothingness is not empty or void; it is a no-thing-ness, this no-thingness is filled to the rim and running over. Because in this realization you realize your true being, your true nature of Oneness with all and in this knowing you are known.

Surrendering

"You were not made to worry...

you were made to fly."

Unless your mind is silent, you cannot know or see your true Self. Your mind is filled with beliefs in you being this and that. As humans, we attach ourselves to beliefs and we demonstrate that belief by fighting to be right. If our beliefs have not yet set us free from suffering, isn't it time to give them up and empty our minds so we may go beyond mind?

If you can observe your thoughts without judgment and without becoming one with them, then you have separated yourself from mind and became the witness to mind.

Normally, when we have thoughts, we become one with that thought and believe it to be true, which then stimulates emotions within us. But when a thought arises and you look at that thought as just a thought, it loses its power over you and you remain in peace.

Believing is seeing. To say one belief is more or less true than another is incorrect. All beliefs are based on lies, but it's hard to convince someone that is actually experiencing it, for the experience is a real experience.

Nothingness is a silent mind. The absence of thoughts, beliefs, ideas and concepts. Zen is not a learning and acquiring of something but a letting go of an unlearning.

The detachment that needs to take place as mentioned in chapter 1 is from the mind, the heart and from the soul.

To detach your true self from the mind, let go of all your beliefs. Surrender them and come to the realization that you truly don't know anything. Everything that you know is knowledge and of this world. This knowledge is subject to change, for we cannot know anything for sure.

We may know for sure that tomorrow the sun may rise, but do we really know that for sure or did we buy into the belief that the sun will rise because it has our whole life? We assume it will rise based on our past experiences, but tomorrow could be the end of the world and the earth stopped rotating or the sun exploded. Yes, these things are very unlikely to happen, but they are nevertheless also possibilities, so we cannot know for sure that the sun will rise.

The second detachment is to detach our true Self from all our attachments. We have attached ourselves to our children, our partners, our parents and so on. Jesus said that if we do not love God more than our parents, we cannot enter the kingdom.

This detachment reminds me of the story of Abraham and how he wanted a child for so many years and then finally, when he got one God asked him to kill his son. Abraham was faced with the hardest decision he ever had to make. Did he love his son or God more? Thank God he did not have to kill his son even though Abraham was ready to.

The whole idea behind this example was not to prove his love for God. It is written that God is a jealous God, but God is not jealous nor does God ask of us anything. The real idea behind this story is for us to understand unconditional love.

If we love someone or something more than something or someone else, we are setting ourselves up for suffering.

That does not mean you shouldn't love your partner or child; it simply means you need to realize the love you have for your child or partner is not unconditional, but conditioned. You may love your child unconditionally, yet it is conditioned to them belonging to you or else you would love all children in this world as much as your own child.

So, the detachment that needs to take place is to hand over all your "belongings." Your child or your partner do not "belong" to you. They have their own spirit and are as free as you are. You may love them and care for them, but they do not "belong" to you. So as with anything you have and are attached to, such as jewelry, cars, houses and so on, these things are for you to enjoy without attachment, and you must realize that they are not your source of happiness.

And last but not least, you need to detach your true Self from your life and that does not mean you commit suicide. To detach your Self from life is to give up ego. This may be harder than you think. With all the negativity we associate the ego, this seems like the easiest to do, but ego is the belief in separation from God. In order to give up ego, you have to surrender your life to God. Hand it over completely. There is no life outside of God. There is no you, me and God. We are One.

You will know if you have truly surrendered your mind, your heart and your soul when you can say and understand the meaning behind the words, "I know nothing, I have nothing and I am nothing."

Death of Ego

"What is Death to Ego...

is Life to Spirit."

The death of ego occurs when we have done the process of undoing or surrendering properly. When a complete and earnest surrendering has taken place and it was not for reasons based on ego's desire to experience something or "get" something out of it, the ego disappears. The death of ego, also known as the dark night of the soul, is an experience of utter emptiness, loss and void. The dark night of the soul is a time where you experience the loss of ego. Since you were attached to ego and believed ego to be your true Self, when ego drops away it feels first like death – and it is: Ego death.

It is not what some think as an act of God who is testing us, but it is rather a life imagined that is coming to an end. We have created images with our beliefs and ideals and gave them value based on how they made us feel or what they reminded us of.

We have put our loved ones above others and now realize that our dearest beloved child is in Truth not closer to us than our worst enemy. Everything we thought was true about us and about the world we live in has come to an end. We realize that we are alone and there is no light whatsoever. We realize that nothing matters. It no longer matters if we are good or bad, or if God loves us, because in this state of being there is no God.

The idea of God is lost with all the other ideas we have bought into over the course of our life.

It is, however, not a suicidal kind of state, but more of a lost state. We are nothing and nothing around us matters. You realize that you have no purpose other than the one you have given to yourself. You realize that you are not the healer, the psychic, the medium or even the enlightened one, but that all these things appeared in the belief of duality.

The death of ego is not for the faint-hearted and it is not something one can look forward to experiencing, yet for those who know it is the dark tunnel we must go through to get to the other side, the death of ego will not scare him away and keep him from walking toward Oneness. He rather does what needs to be done.

For the person who does not know this will happen, this period of time may seem hopeless. It's like the movie *The Matrix* where you took the red pill and woke up to reality, and maybe think you chose the wrong pill and should have gone with the blue pill instead and stayed in ignorance. To the person who does not know that this time of darkness is going to happen, seeks to understand this confusion with his mind and tries to grab whatever is left of ego, for the ground underneath his feet that was built on an imaginary foundation disappeared and he his falling.

Only now does the person (no longer a person) realize how much ego really had to say, not only in our everyday experience, but about everything we perceived through our five senses.

While the state of "darkness" is temporary, it can last for an extended period of time before a new earth dawns and the veil of unknowing is lifted.

Oneness

"In the realization of Oneness,

all illusions disappear."

The path to enlightenment is not truly a path, as a path is something we walk on toward something. Rather, think of enlightenment as your natural state of being and ask yourself what is hindering you from experiencing enlightenment.

If there were a path, it would be one of undoing rather than of doing. You are already everything you hoped to be right now in this very moment but unless this is your awareness it won't be your experience.

Oneness has been called many different names: Self-realization, Enlightenment or clear seeing. It is the goal of all religions and spiritual endeavors.

Once the separation from mind, heart and soul has occurred, one is left in bliss. It does not happen by your doing, however. One day, you the person is there and the next day you wake up and the person is gone and the search is over, for you have found what you have been searching for. What you found, however, is not a thing and therefore very hard to describe in words. It is silence and you realize you are in and one with that silence. The mind's thoughts disappeared and so have the voices we may have heard from God. Where once there was a lot of chatter going on, it is now peaceful awareness without being aware of anything in particular.

You no longer feel alone but realize your oneness with the divine and life itself. Things of this world are still there, but they have lost the meaning you once have given them. They are no longer judged in terms of good or bad but simply by that which causes suffering and that which ends suffering.

At this state of being, you also realize that everyone is already "enlightened." It is a quiet magical awareness, because you see a bigger picture. You understand how everything is in perfect divine order and working toward that goal of manifesting heaven on earth for all.

The real Self is beyond "mind" and therefore it cannot be understood nor grasped by the mind or in terms of knowledge. All knowledge is in and of this world. You can only know the Self by being "it."

Being "it" closes the gap and one is One. As "One," there is no experience and no states of being, for nothing is separate from One. As One even the sense of Self disappears and is absorbed by life itself. It's like a river flowing into an ocean. The river disappears into the mighty ocean.

God is Love, Life and Truth. These three words are symbols for the same thing. If you truly want to know the Truth, you have to separate your true Self from the mind (who you think you are). In "Truth" there is no you, me and God; we are One.

The Witness

"The one who sees thought as
a thought is the witness to mind
and no longer subject to suffering."

Jesus said he was in this world yet not of it. Buddha said something similar when he suggested to be by-passers.

To observe the world as it is in reality is to be the witness. The witness moves through this so called world without thought or judgment. It simply is watching what is going on without interacting even with his thoughts that something is going on. It's like looking through God's eyes.

In the witness state, the mind is silent. There are no thoughts arising in mind and there is no awareness of being the witness either. You can witness a thought once the Self is separated from the mind, but you cannot think you are the witness who is witnessing thought. The minute you realize you are the witness, you are identifying yourself with the mind again and you are no longer the witness. You cannot think or be aware that you are the witness and be the witness at the same time. The minute that thought arises, a separation from being the witness occurs.

As the witness, there is no thought of witnessing. The thought of witnessing is thought and not witnessing. In the witness state the mind is completely silent and if a thought does occur, the witness observes the thought without judgement and without attachment. It just witnesses it without engaging with it.

The difference between witnessing without judgement in comparison to witnessing with judgement is when we observe something happening and we analyze, evaluate and judge what was happening through our mind by recalling situations of the past or what we have learned from others. When we judge and appearance we were one with that happening, we were involved and we were experiencing what was happening around us.

In the witness state there is no experience, there is just witnessing and nothing really happening. Meaning, we are not emotionally nor with our thoughts involved with the appearance of what is happening around us. We simply see it as it is: an appearance in consciousness.

Some may think this means that the enlightened one is heartless, for suffering is still occurring in the world, but this is far from the Truth. The enlightened one keeps his keen mind out of the illusion, so healing may take place. It is a far easier task to give into the appearance and feel sorry for those experiencing suffering, but the enlightened one realizes that no one is helped but giving into the appearance. It is the temptation and belief in duality that is manifesting itself in the physical realm. Help can only come from rising above the appearance.

This does not mean that you no longer help those in need. If those in need are still appearing in your consciousness, you must address it in the physical and look within you to find the lingering belief that is still creating the appearance.

As a witness, you see things as they are and not as they are imagined. Meaning, you see the sky and without labeling it you see it and you can take in its full beauty and magnificence.

Being the witness is like being a child again in awe and wonder of the beauty around us, which has always been around us even before we learned to see it as beautiful and magnificent.

Nothing in the world has changed after enlightenment, but the way you see the world changes everything. You are more aware of the color in the sky and the trees as you pass by. Sometimes your view is large and sometimes zoomed into the bark of a tree, but everything is clear and beautiful and the mind now at peace no longer disturbs our view of this beautiful world all around us. It is like going back to paradise, only now we realize we were in paradise all along but our mind clouded the view.

The Pure Hearted

"Only Love heals, fills your cup to the rim,

includes rather than excludes and gives without

reason or cause."

Those that have a pure heart love unconditionally. Unconditional love cannot be held back from anyone. It is simply that which gives of itself, not because anyone deserves it or needs it. That is simply what unconditional love does.

Even though we as parents would like to think the love between a parent and a child is unconditional, it is not. This kind of love is conditioned based on the child being "ours." If it were unconditional it would include all children of this world. So even though we may love our child unconditionally, it is not unconditional love.

The same is true with partners that have been together for many years.

Unconditional love is not attached nor dependent on an "outside" source. It flows from a well within us all, freely to everyone equally.

The love we have come to know in this world is not unconditional. It is always conditioned because the source from whence it came is conditioned. Love that is conditioned is not of the heart but of the mind and the mind is conditioned. Therefore, anything that comes from mind is also conditioned.

Whenever we speak in terms of relationships, love is conditioned. Only when no relationships are present can love flow freely. Relationships condition the flow. Remove the relationship from the mind, and love flows.

The love that is of the mind is also limited, that is why some people feel taken advantage of once they do favors for others. They expect something in return. Only when you cut off all expectations such as repay, a smile, a thank you or even to be rewarded by "God' are you truly giving from the fullness of your heart. Expect nothing in return. Do it simply for the sake of love, for that is what love does.

In order to love unconditionally, it is best to first fill your own cup to the rim. Unless your own cup is full and running over, you have nothing to share, yet when your cup is full and running over it no longer feels like sharing, it no longer feels like giving or doing good. Once your cup is full and running over, others drink only from the spill.

In order to fill your own cup you must surrender you mind, your heart and your soul so God may fill you with "its" presence and Glory and you are glorified as the true child of God.

To the pure hearted, everyone is equal and they shine their light on the just and unjust. They find compassion with those that don't know what they are doing and as their love seems to go out into the world, it stays within the Oneness of who they are.

In the presence of the pure hearted ones, we feel the presence and ever working nature of God as it unfolds in all things the pure hearted ones come in contact with. We cannot help to feel but a sense of awe and wonder and are uplifted by their presence.

The pure of heart have detached their heart; detached the Self from mind and freed their Soul. They are the free spirited ones that are not afraid to love, for they do not know loss nor fear. They are not afraid to embarrass themselves or make mistakes, for they are free to do so and know no shame. They have no need for secrecy and they do not hide, but are a light unto all. Their life is an open book for their life no longer belongs to themselves, but to the world and all their actions are of God acting in the world constantly pushing the world forward to manifest God's kingdom on earth.

The pure of heart are the true children of God.

www.ingramcontent.com/pod-product-compliance
Lightning Source LLC
Chambersburg PA
CBHW071102040426
42443CB00013B/3377